Magical
JAPAN!

Tokiko Matsudaira

WORKBOOK PRESS LLC
187 E Warm Springs Rd,
Suite B285, Las Vegas, NV 89119, USA

Website: https://workbookpress.com/
Hotline: 1-888-818-4856
Email: admin@workbookpress.com

Ordering Information:
Quantity sales. Special discounts are available on quantity purchases by corporations, associations, and others.
For details, contact the publisher at the address above.

Library of Congress Control Number:
ISBN-13:   978-1-961845-03-9 (Paperback Version)
              978-1-961845-04-6 (Digital Version)

REV. DATE: 05/25/2023

MAGICAL JAPAN

Tokyo, 18th November 2015

Elisabeth and I went to the Nezu shrine. It was a lovely shrine. It depicted Japanese guard dogs guarding the shrine. The stone statues of the dogs were wearing red scarves around their necks. We went by taxi to a Soba restaurant nearby which was a very simple but very charming restaurant. It was a very warm day. We ate cold zaru soba noodles. We poured the stock of the soba noodles into the bowl of sauce dipped the soba noodles in and drank the mixture which was very tasty and very good.

Then we went to Takashimaya in Nihonbashi and I chose a Salvatore Ferregamo small evening bag in black leather to buy as I had left my evening bag in London.

Elisabeth looked for a scarf for herself but was too undecided about them so didn't buy any. We had a club sandwich and corn soup for dinner and had an early night.

Tokyo, 19th November 2015

We went to visit an art gallery holding old fine Japanese prints. They were Ukyoe prints. It was a wonderful collection and most impressive. We went to another noodle shop for lunch. It was crowded there. We had cold soba noodles again with a bowl of prawn tempura. In the afternoon, I had a hairdressing appointment in the hotel, downstairs on the arcade level the hotel. She did my hair very nicely.

In the evening, I wore my new Christian Dior black trousers and a white blouse with black buttons. We ate Chinese food at the hotel. I only had hot and sour soup and Elisabeth had the same soup plus Peking duck skin and we shared a plate of spicy tofu with a bowl of rice each.

That night I was hungry so I got out of bed and ate a bag of pretzels and opened and drank a can of beer. I slept until 5 p.m.

Tokyo, Friday November 20th 2015

Tokyo to Naoshima. Wake up call at 5 am m. I had to be ready to leave from the Otani Hotel to Haneda Airport by 7.30 am m. Quickly ate my breakfast at 6.30 am and finished packing by 7.15 am m. I had to dab some makeup on my face and have the porter bring down my case and extra bag with the duty-free presents in them and check out by 7:30 am. I was a little late but it was all right. We had plenty of time and made it to the airport by 8.15 am. The flight was without incident and we landed at Okayama Airport exactly on time, at 12.20 pm. The car was there and the driver took our luggage and wheeled Elisabeth's extra smaller case to the exit where we were to meet the driver. It took us an hour to get to Uno from Okayama Airport. We took the ferry across to Naoshima. Naoshima's climate is mild and warm. The sea is calm and beautiful and the rolling hills around the island are beautiful.

We went to our rooms and as we had not eaten lunch, we were told the cafeteria in Benesse Museum could offer us refreshments. We took the shuttle bus again to the museum and found the cafeteria and sat down to a lunch of green salad and Elisabeth also had pumpkin soup. We were both very tired.

We returned to the Park Hotel by shuttle bus and did some unpacking though there were no proper closets or drawers.

Most of my clothes were still in the case. It is a beautiful hotel but one must go quite far to reach their restaurants. Elisabeth especially found this exhausting. She went to bed and slept until 6 pm. I knocked on her door and we walked across to the terrace restaurant for dinner. It is located in the hotel. Elisabeth is finding the walking completely exhausting.

Elisabeth said that she went straight to bed after dinner. I got ready for bed as usual and put my clothes away etc and turned off the light at about mmmmmmmm. I slept until 9 am.

Saturday 21st November 2015

Having had a good night's sleep, I went down for breakfast. The food here is very good.

I met Elisabeth on the way to breakfast. This morning, we went by shuttle bus to the Benesse Museum. We saw some very nice modern art paintings from the USA, Britain and of course Japan. It was an impressive collection. We had lunch at the same cafeteria and Elisabeth had Japanese Squid curry and a small plate of salad. I had pumpkin soup and salad. Ice Cream ended our lunch.

After lunch, we went by shuttle bus to the Lee Ufan Museum. We had to pay an entrance fee for this as it was a not part of the Park Hotel Group. We saw sculptures that were beautiful. I bought some postcards of some of their art. It was very Zen. That is what Elisabeth thought. We returned by shuttle bus to the Benesse Museum and waited 15 minutes for another shuttle bus to take us to the hotel. Elisabeth complained to their staff that there was nothing to sit down whilst waiting for the bus. She was right. I sat down on a ledge by the place the bus would stop at.

Tonight, we are going to the Japanese Restaurant at the Benesse Musuem. It means we go back there by bus. There are no buses working after 7pm so we will have to make arrangements with the front desk at the Museum for car and driver to bring us back to the hotel.

Benesse Park Hotel I might add is architecturally a modern building using minimalism as its inspiration. The rooms are very clean and light and spacious. There are no curtains. There is no TV either. I expect it is difficult to obtain a satellite here without ruining the peace of this island.

We went to the Japanese restaurant this evening for dinner. We were served an eight-course meal including dessert. It was very good. One was feeling satisfied after finishing the meal but not stuffed. Congratulations to the chef. The driver picked us up to take us back to the hotel at 8 pm. Then I read about Hiraizumi, the book that Elisabeth gave me. I read the book in bed.

Sunday 22nd November 2015

They have been shooting cleftikos on Charlie Thorpe all day long.

Today we went to the Chio Chu Museum, a 7-minute shuttle ride from the Park Hotel.

The galleries on basement levels 2 and 3. There was a James Turrell work which I liked very much. He uses lighting for all his art. I felt like I was in a lovely cloud, floating in front of a rectangular-shaped light in mauve. It was the closest experience I ever had of being amongst the angels in Heaven.

There were on Level 1, some fabulous Monet paintings, The Water Lilies. It was a big surprise to see them there. We had dinner at the Terrace Restaurant. I had a feeling that Elisabeth was not getting enough sleep as she was being bothered by the British bugs.

Monday 23rd November 2015

Today we spent the day waiting for our flight to take us back to Tokyo. The flight was delayed and we finally got into Tokyo and to our hotel by 7 pm. We quickly put our cases in our room and went up to the Sky Bar and had our drinks. Elisabeth had a

Much-needed gin martini cocktail and I had a glass of champagne. We went down and ate at the Sushi Bar and had a wonderful sushi dinner.

Went to bed earlier and had a good night's sleep apart from Elisabeth who kept getting awakened to talk to the bug.

Tuesday 24th November 2015

I changed some travelers' cheques, some $800. Met the translator and set off by taxi to Tokyo rail station. Just as were leaving, the translator asked us if we had our passports. Elisabeth had forgotten hers. So, we turned back to the Hotel. She went up to her room to get her passport from the case. She eventually came down again, only to tell us she could not find the passport. I went upstairs to her room with her. She could not find the passport. We went down again. We rang the American Embassy. She made an appointment with them, thinking she would have to have a new passport issued. Finally, she tried one more time to look through the case with the translator. She found the passport by her tights and underwear. What a relief! It was already about 11 am. We checked out and left with our cases and passports to Tokyo Station. We got our Japan Rail passes, and reserved our tickets for the various trains we would be taking.

The translator took us after this to Daimaru Department Store where we went to the top floor for a Soba lunch. It was hot in Tokyo, about 22 degrees. We ate cold soba. It tasted very nice.

After this, we went to the platform where we had to catch our train. I don't know what I would have done without the translator. He told us to get off at Utsumiya and go to Platform 5 to catch a local train to Nikko. I am sure I would not have known this if it had not been for him.

We had a comfortable journey all the way and made out change without incident.

We took a taxi to the Kanaya Hotel once in Nikko. We unpacked and rested until 6 am. It is a very nice Hotel and the rooms are spacious with a large window with a large view, although they are both smoking rooms. My room has no smell of smoke. We had a drink at the bar before dinner.

We had their excellent set-course dinner. We had trout. It was delicious. The dining room was very pre-WW2 style. It took Elisabeth back a bit. The dining room was full. After dinner, we went to our rooms and retired for the night.

Wednesday 25th November 2015

I woke up at 5 am. I think that what has disturbed my holiday in Japan this time is the presence of Marie Helvin on our trips. She is a high-powered MI6 spy. They wanted my holiday for her. I have lost a lot of cash recently. Apparently, Marie has no money!

At 10.30 am, we met the taxi driver at the hotel who drove us to Toshogo Shrine where Ieysau Tokugawa is buried. There were various gates that have beautiful coloured carvings. One of the carvings depicted the three wise monkeys who saw no evil, hear no evil, and spoke no evil. Some of the carvings had motifs of leaves. They were sculptured temple guards looking fierce and menacing. There were many stairs in concrete to climb. Elisabeth could not go up to the top where Ieysau's tomb was. There were an awful lot of stairs. I went alone and I had to stop twice to recover my breath and rest my legs standing. At the top, there was a beautiful shrine, and behind the shrine was a simple iron pot. After looking at these, I made my way down. It was a cold day. I took my shoes off to visit other shrines whilst Elisabeth stayed near the shrine with the driver.

Finishing my visit to the shrine, we made our way down a lot of stairs supporting Elisabeth by taking her hand and made our way to the souvenir shop at the bottom where we bought some postcards. We then went to Sawamoto's for lunch where they served barbequed eel on top of rice. We ate this. It was delicious. After lunch, we started our drive to see Kejong Falls. Unfortunately, it was getting very foggy and it started to rain. By the time we arrived, it was too foggy to see anything and it was still raining. We turned back and made our way back to Nikko and our hotel.

After paying our driver, we settled back into our warm and comfortable room for the rest of the day.

Marie had been in my room when I came back from dinner. A solicitor from London had told her to steal my new Christian Dior trousers and white top. I locked these up in my case. I woke up several times in the night. I got up at about 5 am.

Thursday 26th November 2015

I had decided not to leave my new Christian Dior trousers and white top in my case. Will be forced to take them with me or dispose of them whilst I am out of my room for the day. We are going to Mashiko today. It will be a long day for us. It may take 3 hours each way.

Mashiko is a small town. Shoji Hamada had his kiln there beside his spacious and elegant Japanese-style house. We visited his museum. There were artifacts and pottery from ancient times and from other countries. After seeing his museum which housed some of his work, we browsed around shops looking at pottery. I found a mug for Christopher and one for me with the motif of a cat on it. It's very cute. Elisabeth bought a vase, created by a disciple of Shoji Hamada and she also bought a decorative jug. At the noodle shop where we had lunch, they were also selling attractive ceramics. She picked one up for storing her pens and pencils.

After lunch, we went to another museum in Mashiko where we saw more Hamada works as well as the pottery of Togo Messi.

Having looked at the collection, we made our way back to Nikko and stopped at an ATM machine that Elisabeth wanted to use. She eventually succeeded in getting cash.

We returned to the hotel and after unloading our shopping in our rooms, we went directly to the coffee bar via the front desk. I had my 2nd iced coffee latte. I am always falling asleep due to the kleftiko in my left eye.

Friday 27th November 2015

I washed my hair this morning realizing the paler colour of the shampoo was proof that they had put dye into it. The bugs of London are at war with me for unknown reasons if there are any reasons at all. They are determined to make my holiday a right nightmare. I wished them to leave me and Elisabeth alone. I don't know what their problem is but I can't resolve their problems.

Today we leave for Aizu Wakamatsu further north. We decided to visit a museum nearby our hotel as we had time. We were due to leave at 1 pm. We visited the Kasugi Itdem Museum of Art. It was all modern art dating back to pre-WW11 times up to the present day. It was beautiful.

We had a light lunch of sandwiches and coffee at the bar.

The taxi had already arrived so we asked for our luggage and we were off a few minutes past 1 pm. Nearing Aizu Wakamatsu, we passed an area where it was snowing and there was already snow on the ground. It was very pretty to see the snow from the car. Kawabata called it the 'snow country'.

We arrived in Aizu Wakamatsu at about 4 pm. The hotel was a nondescript concrete building. We are on the 9th floor. We met up again at about 6 pm and went to the dining room and each had a glass of Shochu, a Japanese drink you can have with ice as an aperitif or have with a meal. Elisabeth had one but doubt she enjoyed it. We ate a Japanese meal. We avoided eating meat because of an unknown British woman aggressor who kills children for meat. She is, I think a Marie Helvin contact.

Saturday 28th November 2015

Woke up a little later this morning and after a shower went down for breakfast. Had a small amount to eat. I had fruit salad and coffee with cream. At 10 am, the taxi came to fetch us, to take us to Imoriyama, the hill east of the station where the Byokkottai is buried. The Byokkottai were a group of 18 – 19 boys all aged between 15 – 17 years. In 1868, when they heard and saw that the castle had been taken by Government forces, they decided to commit suicide rather than be taken by the enemy. They all died there. On this hill, there is a Pompeian marble column topped by a bronze eagle sent by Rome in 1928 as a salute from the Fascist party to the Byokkottai. They praised their Samuari spirit.

There is a cemetery on the hill as well and a plaque in marble sent from the Nazis to Byokkottai. There was an imprint of a swastika on the plaque but this was removed by the allies later on.

It was easier to go downhill though we took the escalator up and Elisabeth was able to make it to the top! We visited a shrine that had a handmade spiral staircase.

There was a shrine on the top. I went alone as Elisabeth realized she would not be able to climb the spiral staircase with her cane.

We then visited Tsuguro Castle which was last rebuilt in 1965 as a museum. It was first built by Astina Naomori in 1384. It was rebuilt by Ashina Moriuji who made the prototype of the present castle.

A seven-story castle was built in 1591 by Gamo Ujisato. It was called Tsuru Gajo.

In 1611, an earthquake struck and damaged it. Kato Akinori repaired it and made the castle very much like the present one in 1639.

During the Boshin civil war in 1868, in which the imperial army fought the

Tokugawa Shogunate regime. The castle was attacked by the new government which wanted the Meiji restoration and by 1874 the castle was destroyed. By 1934 the castle ruins were declared a national historical site, Wakamaruins was declared a national historical site, Wakamatsugo Castle.

The castle tower was rebuilt on the original site with the support of the local citizens in 1965. The Shogunate Head, Ieysu Tokogawa lived in the castle but there were other famous generals who came and went, not living there but using it to give military orders in times of battle.

Aizu was a location central in importance to the control of Eastern Japan. A castle tower like the one presently standing was built about 400 years ago. About 140 years ago, a terrible war broke out between Aizu and the Meiji Government. The age of the Samuari drew to a close and those Samauri who fought to the end were defeated by the Meiji Government and the castle was destroyed. There was a photo of the castle's restoration which is from the late 19th century and is presumed to have been taken by a Frenchman. We then had lunch at a cafeteria on the castle grounds. We ate a very simple Yakisoba and drank coffee with milk. They had no tea.

We went after lunch to Bukayashiki, the Samauri residence. This was a large house with many rooms and servants' quarters as well. It was a reproduction of the 38-room Samauri Manor which showed feudal life. We also saw a 160-year-old mill. Elisabeth and I went to the shop where she bought a sweet-looking red lacquer box. I was tempted to buy a piece of lacquer myself which is famous in Aizu but thought it was too expensive over 20,000 yen! I still had to pay for the taxi for 6 hours at 5,800 yen per hour! We had a cup of expresso with milk. As I write, it is past midnight and I realize my mistake in having that coffee this afternoon!

We came back with our postcards and Elisabeth's lacquer to the hotel. I eventually went downstairs to reserve a Sushi Soba restaurant by the station for dinner. When we went there, it was busy and friendly. I had sushi and Elisabeth had a nice bowl of Chawan Mushi, miso soup, salad, fruits, and a long plate of Sushi. I had a round plate of sushi with salad and Miso soup. We drank hot Sake. We also had green tea which certainly tasted different from the London green tea.

After dinner, we came back to the hotel. We retired for the night. I switched on my TV and saw the last day of the ice skating Championships presented by NHK Sports. It was wonderful to watch. I watched this as well last year when I was in Japan. It was mainly the men's figure skating I watched then. This year, I watched the woman's figure skating, very exciting. A Japanese girl won 1st prize, followed by an American girl who won 2nd Prize and finally the 3rd prize went to another Japanese girl. In the Men's' Championship, a Japanese boy won a prize exceeding 300 points, he was brilliant.

Monday 30th November 2015

The taxi was waiting for us at 10 am this morning to take us to Hiraizami. We went with a guide who told us the story of Yoshitsune, the younger half-brother of Minamoto Yoritomo, the leader of the Gengi clan. Yoritomo was able to defeat the powerful Heike clan due to the military brilliance of Yoshitsune.

Yoshitsune fell out with Yoritomo who became jealous of Yoshitume's successes. He followed Yoshitsune and eventually exiled him. He was forced to flee Kamakura, with his mistress, Shidzuke and his faithful retainer, Benkei. They disguised themselves as monks to divert the suspicious guards Yoritomo had posted along the roads. At one barrier, a guard became suspicious of one of the monks and Benkei quickly thought of a scheme to alleviate the guards' suspicions. He hit Yoshitsune, his lord, with a staff and pretended to be angry with him. The guard was convinced that Yoshitsune could not be the lord they were searching for. In those days, no retainer dared raise his hand against the person of his lord. Anyway, the guard let the friars pass and they made their way to Hiraizumi where a friendly lord of the Fujiwara clan had his stronghold. The old lord Hidenara protected Yoshitsune, but after he died his son became fearful of Yoritomo's wrath. Yoshihara yielded to Yoritomo's threats and attacked Yoshitsune at the Takadashi. Yasuhara betrayed his father's friends and Yoshitsune and his retainers were murdered in Hiraizumi in 1689. However, this did not save the Fujiwara of Hiraizumi from Yoritomo.

The same year, he marched north and destroyed this most important remaining centre of military power. With the end of Hiraizumi, Japan was under the rule of one military leader.

Later on in the 17th Century, a famous Heiku poet visited the Takadashi. He was Batsuo Basho. This was done to commemorate the 500 anniversaries of Yoshitsune's death.

There is a shrine of Yoshistune with a wooden statue of him. From the Takadashi, one has a view of the Kitakami River below, Mount Tabashine in the distance and River Keiome on the left. There is also Benkei Hall. By the tower of Hirazumi in a quiet spot by a tree lies the body of Benke. There is a black marble memorial plaque there as well. We did not visit Benkei's shrine as the road was too steep to climb for Elisabeth so she said she would wait for us but as it was a distance to get there and back, we canceled it and I would have to see it another time. It was also very cold. Japan is in winter now and we are in the north of Japan which is very cold at the moment, even if the sun shines.

We visited the museum which has four parts to it, Chusonji, Hondo, Sankozo, and Corijido. The Chusenji hold sutras which are written on dark blue paper in alternating silver and gold lines. Hondo holds memorial services in front of Shaka Nyrizi – historical buddah and Zazen meditation.

Sankozo has more than 3000 national treasures and important cultural assets. One can see sutras, documents, objects, and Fujiwara clan burial accouterments exhibited in the rooms.

Konjokido – Goldenhall was completed in 1124. It is unique. One can see the statue of Amida Nyorai – the Buddha of infinite light with canon – the Buddhisatire of compassion or the right Seishi, the Buddhisatire of wisdom - on the left.

Sina Jizoboddhisatire – survivors from hell and two guardian kings, Jikokutan and Zochotan stand in front. The Hall is covered with gold leaf which represents the radiant western pure land – Gokuraka or the land of utmost bliss.

The inner sanctuary, lavishly decorated with Mother of Pearl, Maki – E 'gold sprinkled liqueur and elaborate carving is the height of Heian 12th Century Buddhist Art.

The remains of the 4 lords of 4 generations of Fujiwara are laid to rest beneath the central altar, the 3rd lord with the 4th lord, Yasuhera, beneath the right altar.

The first Lord was Kiyohira, the 2nd was Motohira, the 3rd was Hidehira and the 4th lord was Yasuhira.

We walked around a pond. There used to be residences and shrines around it but they were burnt down by the fire. The stone markings on the ground are all that remains of the villas.

The pond was like a perfect glass that reflected the sky, the trees, and the rocks standing in the pond. The views from the angles around the pond were quite beautiful.

Our tour ended here. We went to see Yoshitsune's shrine and see where Hidehira had his house. It was a most impressive tour though the weather was cold. The guide couldn't have been better. He did a good job showing us Hiraizumi.

The descriptions of the empty spaces where the villas once stood around the pond are called Mats – Ji is a world heritage site. Benkei was my father's favourite hero. It would be great if one day soon I could visit his small shrine in Hiraizumi.

I would do it for my father!

1st December 2015

Today we decided to hire a taxi for 5 hours and go to Oshu City, about one hour from Inchinoseki. Once there, we visited 3 museums at Choei Memorial Museum. Saito Makoto Memorial Museum and Goto Champi Memorial Museum, Takano Choei Memorial Musuem was western culture scholar at the end of the Edo period, when Japan was still closed to foreign contact. He wanted Japan to open itself to the world. He was oppressed by the Tokugawa Bafuka Government. He was put into prison for his outspokenness. The museum shows portraits of him as well as letters and documents and a piece of his prison uniform. Sito Makoto – 1858 – 1936 was the 30th Prime Minister of Japan who was assassinated during the February 26th incident of 1930. He was a friend of the Navy having done his military service in it. He opposed the Nanking War in China and the Military retaliated. The Musuem was built on the Sito Family's estate where the old residence has been preserved and is open to the General Public. The Museum exhibits his medals and a cracked mirror damaged at the time of his assassination. Goto Shimpei – 1857 to 1929 was a Japanese Statesman who served in many posts such as the 7th Mayor of Tokyo, the Home Minister of Japan, the 1st Minister of Tokyo Broadcasting Corporation, and the 1st Chief Scout of Japan.

He had also studied medicine in Germany. He helped reconstruct Tokyo after the great Kanto earthquake. We tried to visit Kikuta Kazuo Memorial Museum but it was closed. He was a famous playwright. We also tried to visit the Maji Museum but this was closed today. We traveled a few miles south of Oshu City and found our way to the Cupola. They showed iron works and it was displayed for sale in their giftshop as art. Elisabeth bought a very sweet red painted iron paperweight and I bought a red mask of Kabuki, also a paperweight. We returned to Inchinoseki after this and I bought a Coke Zero from the vending machine, outside our hotel. I quenched my thirst in my room. Tonight, we will return to Elisabeth's favourite restaurant the one we went to the first night. She wants to see the waitress again who is very friendly and very nice.

Wednesday 2nd December 2015

Today we made our way to Inchiniseki Train station at 10 am. Our train was not due to depart until 11.48 am. We asked the front desk for help to walk across the station with our heavy luggage. The receptionist took us across to the station. It was very cold and he had no overcoat. He got us to the right platform which was a complicated maneuver. We sat on the side and waited for our train. It was not the bullet train we had expected to be on. We stopped at every station. However, the seats were very comfortable.

We arrived in Tokyo at about 2 pm. We found our way to

the exit and to the taxis. We taxied our way back to New Otani Hotel.

That evening we had sushi in the Sushi Restaurant in the main building. We had an early night.

Thursday 3rd December 2015

Today we tried to see the Matsudaira Gardens, Hama – Rikyu Gardens it rained. I had my rain hat on but Elisabeth had not brought her umbrella and hat so we turned back. We eventually caught a taxi and asked him to take us to the folklore Arts and Crafts museum which was very far away. After driving for at least half an hour - 45 minutes we arrived there to find it was closed. So we headed back to the hotel. We had lunch at the café and a Japanese-style hamburger which was very good.

It was still raining so after lunch we went downstairs to the Arcade level and browsed around the shops.

We went to our room and about 15 minutes later, the Hotel management rang my door and asked if he could disinfect my room. They stayed for about 5 minutes. They disinfected my owl! In the evening, we went to Akira's Restaurant in Akashaka called Zakura. We had Sukiyaki though Elisabeth did not particularly want it. They served Matsuzaki beef and a delicious plate it was. Elisabeth loved ice cream, probably even more than me. We had ice cream for dessert. We went back to the hotel and had an early night.

Friday 4th December 2015

We caught the train from Kanazawara this morning. It is always such a performance to find the right track. Most people working in the station understand English and speak a little. The train stopped about 5 times and they did not put us into the bullet train. We went 1ˢᵗ class and the seats were comfortable. We took a taxi at Kanazawa Rail Station and found our way with some difficulty to our Hotel, the Ana Crown Plaza. The Hotel was a lot cleaner than what I remembered of it the year before.

We went to the Chinese Restaurant for dinner and had a good meal. I had prawns with vegetables. Elisabeth had crab meat and greens. I also ordered tofu with minced pork and chili sauce. This was delicious. We drank Kiran beer. We returned to our rooms after dinner.

Saturday 5ᵗʰ December 2015

We met up with Yoshiko Hayakawa a few minutes before 11 am. The taxi was waiting for us. He drove us to Myokeji Temple and there we were met by the temple priest and his wife. I gave the bottle of champagne to Mr. Uchida who seemed pleased to receive it. Must ask Akira if gift-giving is allowed here.

After a good session with him over a cup of Japanese Green tea, we prayed by the tombstone of Grandpa and the priest chanted a religious song. We put flowers by his graveside and Elisabeth had bought a few chrysanthemums as well. It had stopped raining.

After this, we said our goodbyes to Mr. and Mrs. Uchida and went off to a very fine restaurant for lunch. It was an old building that had been refurbished inside. We sat at a table with chairs. We had many different courses. They were very small servings. However, we were quite full after the meal.

After this, we went to the Museum of Contemporary Arts. It was extremely crowded. Yoshiko said this was because of the new bullet train. There were many young people. We saw the permanent collection which is free. There was a James Tully. As usual, it was wonderful. I bought some postcards of the other artworks we saw.

We decided to leave. It would have been a bit of a wait to see the Payne Collection because of the long queue. Yoshiko took us to the Samurai District of Kanazawa which is quite near the temple. We went browsing around the shops in the Samurai Quarter and admired their Kutani porcelain.

Then we went to Samurai's residence with a beautiful garden. We went up the stairs and saw the private quarters. There is a shrine in the house. We gazed at the garden from the terrace balcony.

#

Then we returned to the Hotel. Before we set off, we went to a convenience store to buy some hard sweets for me. They aren't at all bad and something to suck. After we had arrived back at the Hotel, I paid the taxi driver. That evening, we had a light meal of soup and salad and a scoop of ice cream.

6th December 2015

This evening we met up with an old friend of mine called Yoko. She is a teacher teaching young children. As we hadn't met for several years, we had a lot to catch up on. Always the lady, Elisabeth was most impressed by her politeness. We took her to the Sushi Bar and ate our dinner there. It may be a long time before we meet again.

www.ingramcontent.com/pod-product-compliance
Lightning Source LLC
Chambersburg PA
CBHW051605120626
46551CB00013B/1672